Community In The Face of Tragedy

ELEANOR'S HOUSE

Aunt Edna,

To God be all the glory,

Great things He is doing!

Ken

Ken Penner

FriesenPress

Suite 300 - 990 Fort St
Victoria, BC, v8v 3K2
Canada

www.friesenpress.com

Additional Contributors:
Interior News (Illustrator)
Navigators (Illustrator)

ISBN
978-1-5255-7224-1 (Hardcover)
978-1-5255-7225-8 (Paperback)
978-1-5255-7226-5 (eBook)

1. RELIGION, CHRISTIAN LIFE, INSPIRATIONAL

Distributed to the trade by The Ingram Book Company

Table of Contents

Dedication

This book is dedicated to Almighty God, Creator of heaven and earth, the God who is love, who gives his love to us so that we can love others as he first loved us! "God showed how much he loved us by sending his one and only Son into the world so that we might have eternal life through him. This is real love—not that we loved God, but that he loved us and sent his Son as a sacrifice to take away our sins. Dear friends, since God loved us that much, we surely ought to love each other." (1 John 4:9–11)

Introduction

With wars, conflicts, and disasters all around us, we could easily become disillusioned. Yet at times we see people do amazing things just to help someone in the middle of adversity. Newscasts are full of negative stories about stealing, killing, and destroying, so it's refreshing to hear about people rallying together to help one another in a time of difficulty and need.

I want to let you in on a secret: there's a place where the people are exceptional, and these people have influence around the world, extending to such places as Cambodia, Mexico, Guatemala, Sudan, Uganda, Finland, Nepal, Greenland, and Russia. However, I didn't write this book to focus on their generosity far and wide—I'll leave that for another time, another place, another book. Let's focus for a short time on the love these people have for their own neighbours.

I believe the following is an example of what God would want for all of us, all the time. As Jesus said, we should "Love your neighbor as yourself" (Luke 10:27), and "Do to others as you would like them to do to you" (Luke 6:31). What a different world it would be if we practised these principles!

In the following pages, you'll read about the true experiences of neighbours reaching out in love to a woman with a desperate need, one she couldn't fulfill herself. Only as many others came together could her need for shelter and a home be met. In the meeting of this need, no single person stands out. Many people were needed, and many people were involved. Numerous people from far and near each played a part. God had a plan, and he used people to accomplish it.

Jesus taught that our neighbour is not only the one located in close proximity to us, but the one who shows mercy and help (Luke 10:30–37). As we follow the Lord's leading, we become his hands and feet!

This is a true account of what actually happened in the Bulkley Valley of Northwestern British Columbia, Canada. It's impossible to name all those who helped. Many silently and anonymously reached out, incognito as it were, not wanting their names to be known, even at times, to the recipient. Some gave more than others, but some who gave a "little" actually sacrificed the most (Luke 21:1–4)! The amount given is not for us to measure—obedience is what's important, not a measure of how much we or others have done. This is one reason why I'm writing this testimony of the faithfulness of Eleanor's neighbours. All felt compelled to help this wonderful lady, and I feel led to write this down as a record that can be shared for generations to come.

I have decided not to use actual names but descriptors for most of those mentioned in this story. To name all involved would be impossible, and some of the greatest givers may not even be mentioned.

The following is a brief and incomplete review of this amazing experience, from my point of view. Each person involved, or even looking on from the sidelines, will have a different perspective. The events, people, and situations mentioned here are accurate to the best of my memory, and I take full responsibility for any errors present in the narrative.

An alphabetical list of those we know of who gave of materials, finances, and time is included in the Appendix. Even this isn't a complete list, so please know that if you contributed but are not on the list, you weren't left out intentionally. God knows who you are, and your reward ultimately lies with him.

I believe God initiated and was involved in this whole experience. After reading about some of the amazing events and people involved, I think you'll agree that it was a work of God from beginning to end. I must give God all the glory, as he's the one who made us and gives us life, breath, and all things (Acts 17:25). To whom else could we give the honour and glory? Certainly, there is no room for giving glory to ourselves!

I also would have liked to remain anonymous, but after being advised by others whose counsel I trust, I felt that to take responsibility for what is written, I should let my name be put on this work. I also felt it was important to have Eleanor's name in the text, and I've done so with her permission.

I have included some scripture references throughout the book for those who may be encouraged by them, especially those of the Christian faith. To express the amazing provision of God throughout the project, and even in this writing, I felt, as a Christian believer, compelled to include them. At the end of each chapter I have included a few questions regarding why we should reach out in this way.

Hopefully all can be encouraged by this attempt to record some memorable history of a remarkable people in a special place, so that we can be reminded of what can happen when we obey the call to "Do to others whatever you would like them to do to you" (Matthew 7:12a).

Questions to Consider

1. Why is there so much conflict, such as racism, hate, and war, in the world today? What might be the root cause of such behaviour?

2. What are some of the ways in which people can influence others for good, whether in our neighbourhood, country, or world? Can you think of some examples?

3. What do Jesus' words, "Do to others whatever you would like them to do to you," mean to you? If this were our creed, what effect would it have on the conflicts that arise in our communities, country, and world?

4. How does a community effort in helping those in need compare to an individual effort? How does the individual's attitude affect the community's corporate attitude toward helping others? What are some of the dynamics of individual outreach? Of community outreach?

5. Why might some of those who reach out to help others want to remain anonymous? Why might others want their work to be made known?

Chapter 1

BAPTISM BY WATER

We met Eleanor for the first time at a weekly Bible fellowship in the home of "Mom Penner" in Quick, British Columbia.* As Eleanor lived nearby, she attended these meetings on a fairly regular basis. As we got to know her, we found her to be a friendly, congenial, independent person with the spirit of a survivor. We learned that she worked hard at her farm, eking out a living by raising sheep and llamas and tending a garden. She had recently decided to scale down the farming activity and semi-retire.

Eleanor had lived on her property since 1969. Over the years, she always made sure that she had plenty of extra

---

* Mom Penner had "adopted" us.

things on hand, including hot water tanks, roofing materials, knitting machines, propane tanks, and whatever else she thought she might need in the future. She always gathered things, just in case. You never know when something might fail and you need that very thing you bought at the garage sale a few weeks ago. I can understand this, because I do the same thing. We have lots of stuff stored up in the back yard, just in case! Anyone who knew Eleanor knew she had lots of stuff, just in case!

The time came when we were no longer able to meet at Mom's place, as she passed on to be with the Lord. Mom's daughter (my "adopted" sister) and her husband sold their place and moved away to Terrace. Subsequently, Mom's place was sold too. Before moving, my adopted sister wanted to be baptized in the Skeena River and asked if I could perform the baptism. Eleanor heard about it and said she wanted to be baptized at the same time as my sister. It was freezing cold at the time, and none of us wanted to enter the frigid waters of the river, which often froze over completely in the short, frigid days of our northern winters. So we decided to wait until more balmy weather came upon this wonderful piece of God's creation in Northwestern BC.

We agreed upon August 15, 2010, which turned out to be a beautiful sunny day. Some friends and relatives came, and we made our way to the river, which ran just past my brother and sister's back yard. We found a back eddy of the river that worked just fine for our purposes. After some hearty singing, prayer, and a few words, both Eleanor and my sister were baptized in water that day.

Adult water baptism is a time when a believer proclaims publicly their faith and new life in Jesus Christ. The immersion in water and subsequent rising up symbolizes the death, burial, and resurrection of Jesus Christ and the person's identification with Christ. The person being baptized is proclaiming, through faith in Jesus Christ, that they have died to their old life and been born again spiritually to a new life given to them by Christ Jesus. It's a celebration of having one's sins washed away through the death of Jesus and living the new life he promised to everyone who believed in him (John 1:12). It was this new life in Jesus that both Eleanor and my sister witnessed to that day.

We enjoyed a wonderful time of fellowship after the baptism. The weather was warm, the sun was shining, and the ground was very dry, as it hadn't rained for some time. We rejoiced and thanked God for his undeserved favour upon us all.

Little did we know what would happen just a few days later.

Questions to Consider

1. What does baptism mean to you?

2. Does one receive baptism to get right with God, or is it evidence of being right with God?

3. Is God more interested in outward actions or the condition of the heart?

4. How does the condition of the heart affect our outward actions?

5. How would our answer to the question above impact our view of baptism and our perspective on our relationship with God?

6. Are there baptisms other than water baptism?

Chapter 2

BAPTISM BY FIRE

She was awakened by a bang on her door. To this day, she's not sure what caused the bang. Eleanor went to the door and found it open, but nobody was there.

In the distance, she could see smoke and flames, fanned by the wind, licking up under the power and telephone lines across the road. She tried to phone the Forest Service, but her cordless phone didn't work, as the power was now out. She plugged a landline-type phone into the phone jack and was able to call out with it. She told the Forest Service that there was a fire near her home. They informed her that they already had water bombers in the air, flying over her place, due to an existing fire in the nearby Houston area.[*]

The wind was blowing strongly on August 18, and the trees and vegetation were tinder-dry. The fire hazard was high, as there had been very little rain in the past month or so. As it happened, the wind blew so hard that it uprooted a tree, which fell onto the power line just across the road from Eleanor's place. As Eleanor was taking an afternoon nap, the tree shorted out against the power line, producing sparks that fell onto the ground and tinder-dry grass beneath the power line. In a very short time, the wind whipped up the sparks into flames. Nearby scrub brush and trees were set on fire. As Eleanor slept, the brisk wind blew airborne embers across the road onto her property.

Eleanor is a survivor with an independent streak. She cut her own firewood with her electric chainsaw, and she knew how to take care of herself! She wasn't about to let a forest fire burn her place down! She tried to run a water hose but the power was off, so her water pump in the well couldn't function, meaning that no water came out of the hose. She turned to her rainwater barrels and dipped a small pail into the water to try to douse the quickly-expanding fire.

At that point, her neighbour from across Highway 16 arrived on the scene. He saw that the fire had spread into the dry grass behind Eleanor's house and that it would be

---

[*] The fact that there was already an existing fire in the Houston area was a Godsend. The BC Forest Service was already in high gear with initial attack crews, firefighting equipment, and water bombers in the region, ready to help put out the fire on Eleanor's property on fairly short notice.

impossible to put it out with just a pail of water from a rain barrel! Fearing the inevitable, he convinced Eleanor to leave her place. She jumped into her van and backed out of the driveway just as the flames circled around her large, recently-filled propane tank. The fire was rapidly heading for her mobile home.

Meanwhile, some of the neighbours came to help put out the fire; one offered his bulldozer to make a fire guard behind her place, but the Forestry personnel already on the scene would not allow them to, as the water bombers were coming and everyone had to clear out. Eleanor and her neighbours watched as her old log workshop, home, and everything she owned went up in smoke. The neighbour from across Highway 16 remembers seeing the sheet metal from her roof fly thirty feet in the air as the flames were whipped up by the wind. The water bombers came too late to save Eleanor's place, but they averted a massive fire that could have consumed much of the neighbouring properties.

For the sake of public safety, Highway 16 was shut down for a couple of hours as the water bombers attacked the fire. Some said seven bombers dropped their fire retardant on the property, while others claimed as many as thirteen, but the inferno was well doused and contained by late evening. It took another week before the Forest Service mop-up crews extinguished all the smoldering embers. All that was left was the twisted, heat-marred metal that resisted being consumed by the flames. Ditches in her field were left by the fire suppression crews, giving evidence of their work in chasing the fire, even underground, to finally put it out.

The next day when I heard that the fire had consumed Eleanor's home, I thought, *She was just baptized a few days ago. What is she going to think of God now? How could he have let this happen, especially at this time, when she had just dedicated her life to him by being baptized?*

I contacted Eleanor, and we got together to discuss what had happened and what we were going to do about it. After she shared about her narrow escape with death and the loss of her earthly home, we spoke of her baptism. I asked her, "What do you think God is trying to say by allowing this to happen to you?"

She had obviously already been thinking along these lines, as she quickly answered, "I think God gave me a kick in the seat of my pants to help me change my lifestyle."

To me, this was a profound statement, showing wisdom that could only come from the Lord. It also demonstrated that he had given her a new direction, even through this tragedy. She had an amazing sense of peace about it all, which I initially attributed to shock. *She'll probably see it a bit differently as the shock wears off,* I thought. But this sense of peace followed her throughout the ordeal from beginning to end. Now I know it was the Lord (Philippians 4:7).

Questions to Consider

1. How could this fire be seen as a baptism?

2. If God is a good God, why would he allow this to happen?

3. How were Eleanor's neighbours a help to her on the tragic day of the fire?

4. Can you imagine how Eleanor felt when, right before her eyes, everything she owned and had worked for went up in smoke?

5. What do you think Eleanor meant when she said, "I think God gave me a kick in the seat of my pants to help me change my lifestyle?"

6. What might be some other ways in which God might help us to change our lifestyles?

Chapter 3

THE AFTERMATH

It was almost a week before we could check through the twisted metal and hot ashes for valuables that might have escaped the flames. Eleanor wanted to know if we could find her "fireproof" safety deposit box, which contained some valuable papers and some coins from her coin collection. As we sifted through the ashes, the heat of the ground through our footwear and the acrid smell of the ashes were a constant, eerie reminder of the disaster that had happened only a week earlier. We found only half of the safety deposit box, which had been almost completely consumed by the scorching blaze. We did find some coins melted together, and some that were more recognizable but definitely thoroughly tempered and discoloured by the inferno and intense heat. We also rescued a hammer and a few other things from the ashes.

Aftermath of fire. (Picture courtesy E. Bennett)

Eleanor was looking after a mobile home for some caring friends near her place at the time of the fire. They were away for an extended period of time, so she phoned them and told them what had happened. They offered their home for her to stay until things were sorted out. As it turned out, she was blessed to stay there for the better part of a year.

Eleanor went to a local law office in Smithers to get a copy of her will, as her copy had burned up in her fireproof safety deposit box. This helpful lawyer was very sympathetic to her and offered his expertise wherever he could. Before she left his office, he gave her a computer so that she could stay connected with others via the internet.

The next day, we decided to go to the local credit union to ask them to open a trust fund account so that people could donate to Eleanor, as many were already asking how they could help. The credit union personnel were very understanding and thoughtful. They suggested that we go to the local radio station and newspaper with her story, so we went to the radio station just across the road. Having already heard of the tragedy, they were very compassionate and interviewed Eleanor. Many listeners told me they heard the interview and were touched in their heart as Eleanor bravely and in a wavering voice recounted her brush with death and the harrowing experience of only a couple of days before. Eleanor couldn't help but laugh at times, which I think was due to the shock, but she said she knew it was no laughing matter and that the full reality of it would hit home sooner or later.

Next, we went to the local newspaper. It seemed as if they'd been waiting for her. The editor immediately interviewed her. One of their reporters had been at the fire and had taken pictures, so now the interview filled in the details. The story hit the front page of the paper.

THE INTERIOR NEWS

103RD YEAR · WEEK 33   SMITHERS, B.C.   WEDNESDAY, AUGUST 25, 2010   interior-news.com   SINGLE COPY · $1.34 ($1.20 + 14¢ HST)

SPRAY DOWN

Cameron Orr/Interior News

Crews hose down the remains of a fire that began when a tree hit a power line last Wednesday evening. Tragically lost in the blaze was Eleanore Bennett's home. She had lived on the property since 1969.

Quick home lost

By Cameron Orr
Quick/Interior News

"I heard a noise." That's how the story begins for Eleanore Bennett, 71, a homeowner on Wakefield Road in Quick.

That noise was the sound of the wind blowing her door open on August 18. And that lead her to discover bad news coming her way.

"I go to close my door and then I see the smoke and the flames on the trees across the road and I thought, 'Oh...'"

Bennett was in a remarkably good mood the day after her home burned down, cracking jokes as she talked to *The Interior News*.

Even as the fires burned her home she was making quips to her neighbours.

"This wasn't really the way I was thinking about getting rid of all the stuff that's in my house and my trailer," she said at the time.

She knows that the jokes are just how she is coping with the trauma, and she fully expects not to be so happy one day.

"I laugh about it," she said. "One of these days I'm not going to be laughing, I'm going to be screaming and yelling."

> **One of these days I'm not going to be laughing**
>
> — *Eleanore Bennett*

Her home went up in smoke during a small wildfire which erupted when a tree hit a power line across from her property.

Winds carried the flames cast before changing direction and lighting her own grass fields.

See FIRE *on Page A2*

Front page of Interior News, August 25, 2010.
(Article and pictures courtesy Interior News)

PAGE A2 - THE INTERIOR NEWS - WEDNESDAY, AUGUST 25, 2010

NEWS

Donation account means public can give help

FIRE *from Page A1*

She said it was approximately 4:30 p.m. when she saw the fire, but she had to find her corded phone before she could make the call – the power had gone out, causing her cordless phone to not work.

Kim Steinbart, fire information officer with the Northwest Fire Centre, said that their office received the call at about five o'clock and air tankers were deployed right away.

In fact an air tanker was already flying in the vicinity when the call came in.

"It was one of those situations where it happened to be in the right place at the right time."

She said tankers dropped flame retardant around the perimeter of the fire to prevent it from spreading.

In total the fire was six hectares.

Highway 16 was also closed for approximately two hours while crews worked on the fire.

Steinbart said that safety was one reason for the closure – people were stopping to watch the fire, causing a hazard on the road. The closure was also in case some retardant spilled onto the highway. The substance can be quite slippery.

The road reopened around 7:30 that evening.

Eleanore's home was the only one lost in the fire.

Among her many possessions damaged or destroyed was a safety deposit box which contained vintage coins – some from the 1890s and others from her father when he was overseas.

The material is still there, but they've all melted together.

"They're kind of all mushed together now. I don't know what to do with them."

The fire didn't win without a fight. Elea-

Cameron Orr/The Interior News

Eleanore Bennett's property still smolders days after a wildfire in Quick.

nore was out in her field throwing buckets of water at the fire in an attempt to keep it at bay.

And she would have stood her ground longer if not for her neighbour.

"My neighbour came over and said, 'you gotta get out of here.' I said, 'We gotta get this fire out.'"

Her neighbour won the argument and Eleanore grabbed her purse, some shoes, and drove her van off her property and simply watched the fire take her home from Hatch Road.

Afterwards, there was nothing left.

"We walked to the edge of my driveway and all I could see was smoke where it used to be my trailer."

Friends immediately rallied for her support. She is living at a friends home and neighbours have been bringing her food and taking her into town for shopping.

Friends and the public are welcome to support her through an account at the Bulkley Valley Credit Union. At any of their four branches people can request to make a deposit to the Eleanore Bennett Donation Fund.

Eleanore had lived at her home since September 1969.

Newspaper article August 25, 2010, continued.
(Article and pictures courtesy Interior News)

Immediately after the fire, many of Eleanor's neighbours came over to see her. People brought food, dishes, and pots and pans. Many of her immediate needs were met due to the generosity of her neighbours. Some donated money toward her trust. Eleanor kept these funds in this account to hopefully build something in the future.

Our attempt to get help for her from the government was, to say the least, challenging, drawn out, and disappointing.

In the end, it proved futile. We applied to the Provincial Emergency Disaster Relief Program, who initially said she wouldn't get funding because she hadn't been ordered out of her house by the government. We countered that she had been ordered out by the Forest Service personnel when the bombers came. Next we received a letter from them stating that because she didn't have insurance, she didn't qualify for disaster relief. We explained that she'd been denied insurance in 1986, but that letter had been burned in the fire. We attempted to get a copy of the letter, but the insurance company didn't keep files that far back, so it was impossible to prove.

We went back to the helpful lawyer for advice, and he suggested that we get a quote for insurance on the pre-fire dwelling. Her previous insurance company wouldn't do it for her, but the insurance company across the road from the credit union did. The quote for an annual premium was at a minimum 20 per cent of her very limited income, which made it impossible for her to have procured insurance. The helpful lawyer sent a letter to the disaster relief people, but they said that they couldn't help.

We went to the BC provincial ombudsman to see if there was anything they could do, but they came back with a different answer than all the other agencies: the fire had not been approved as a disaster by the legislature, so no relief was available. Eleanor then approached the local MLA for help. There were handshakes and words of sympathy, but she never got one call from their office, even though they said they would be in touch with her soon. Trying to get relief from the government was becoming tedious, and it became obvious that the government had dug in their heels and there would be no help from them.

Even though we faced these initial disappointments, the locals from the neighbourhood encouraged us, as many asked, "What are we going to do with Eleanor? How can we help?"

Being a believer in a personal God who cares about every detail of our lives, I spent time praying about this situation, yet it all seemed so impossible. When we'd been looking through the ashes shortly after the fire, her neighbour from across Highway 16 had come over and suggested that we build her a shack so she could have a place to live. This was on my mind as I prayed for direction. "What should we do, Lord?"

Some talked about suing the power company, because the fire had started with their power line, but the helpful lawyer thought that would be a very drawn out, expensive process with no guarantee of results. Eleanor agreed.

I asked Eleanor what she wanted to do. We talked about applying for accommodation in a seniors' complex, possibly finding a used mobile home to put on the property, or maybe even building a small house there. After thinking about it, Eleanor said that she wasn't ready for seniors' accommodation, and that seeing her mobile home burn up so quickly made her fearful of another fire. She felt she would like a small house to live in. I asked her to come up with a sketch of a floor layout to meet her needs. She went on the internet and found a practical yet simple plan of a cozy little place.

Some of my thoughts at the time included: *How will we go about this? It seems like such a large project with no insurance and no government help. If we start, will we have the resources to complete it? A half-built house is just as useless as no house at all.*

At times it seemed quite overwhelming. Maybe we could just find a place for Eleanor to live in town. Maybe she could just sell her property and put a down payment on something else. But as I prayed about it, I always came back to the words of Jesus: "Do to others whatever you would like them to do to you" (Matthew 7:12a).

I contacted a local general contractor who had helped build an addition onto our house the previous fall and asked him about possibilities. He looked at the sketches and said it would cost possibly $80,000 to build. I then asked him to come out to see the site, and he, Eleanor, and I met there. He said we might need a new sewer system as well, as this was a new house. That would cost another $25,000. This project was getting bigger all the time! The general contractor agreed, at no cost, to draw up some detailed plans for the building and suggested some changes. We ended up with a small house of 720 square feet.

It was a trying time through the winter of 2010/2011. All the avenues we had pursued were dead ends, but we had a house plan and a figure as to the cost to build it!

Questions to Consider

1. Does "fireproof" necessarily mean fireproof when used in advertising a product? What does this say about warranties, insurance, and guarantees of people and corporations?

2. Do you think it was a coincidence that Eleanor's caring friends were away for an extended period of time, allowing her to stay at their home?

3. Do lawyers usually give away their computers? What might have motivated the helpful lawyer, the radio station, and the neighbours to be so helpful?

4. Is it the duty of the government to take care of everyone's needs? If they don't, who will?

5. Are there situations in which buying insurance is not a good idea?

6. Should our response to those in tragic circumstances be dependent upon whether or not they have insurance?

7. What was the power company's responsibility in this? Would it have been wise to sue the power company?

8. What kind of response would you have liked if you were in Eleanor's situation?

Chapter 4

"DO TO OTHERS"

These words of Jesus as recorded in the Bible—"Do to others whatever you would like them to do to you" (Matthew 7:12a)—would come to me whenever we prayed for Eleanor and her situation. *If one was in Eleanor's predicament*, I thought, *what would one want? Would I like to be forced into the old age home when I'm perfectly capable of living on my own? Would I like to be left alone to work it out myself? Would I like to have an old mobile home to live in, even if I was afraid when I thought of my last one going up in smoke? Would I like to be criticized by people for not buying insurance, which I couldn't afford?* It became obvious to me that what I would like is what Eleanor desired: to have a house built, in which I could enjoy life and see the hand of God taking care of me.

The questions continued to swirl through my mind: *How are we going to go about this? This is a big project. If we start, will it get completed?* Yet "Do to others" kept going through my mind.

So it was settled. We would build a house for Eleanor, and God would cause it to happen. When I thought about all that had to happen, I felt like running. But it was clear—we needed to obey the calling to do unto others.

It was obvious that no matter what, the site had to be cleaned up. I contacted a friend from Houston who, just after the fire, had mentioned he would like to help out, possibly with his backhoe or something. We met on the site, and as we kicked the ashes around, we discussed what had to be done. We discussed all the possible options. I valued his judgement, as he also was a man of faith. After we had conversed for a bit, he said, "The only right thing to do is to build her the house." This was a definite confirmation for me. We were going ahead!

My friend said he thought we needed an excavator with a thumb on it to get rid of all the metal and debris, so he would talk to an equipment supplier in Houston to see if they would donate one for a few days. He also arranged for a church youth group to come out and gather the smaller pieces of steel that the excavator would have difficulty picking up. Along with this, he asked a salvage company to bring out a bin that we could put the steel in. Eleanor had already gone through the ashes and retrieved what little there was and was okay with us starting to clean up the site.

My friend and about twenty-five members of the church youth group showed up one evening and eagerly and efficiently made a quick job of cleaning up the smaller pieces of metal. They had fun doing it too! Eleanor was there working alongside them, and it was wonderful to see. Everyone got dirty, but it was great to see these youth willing to serve in this way.

The general contractor made up a materials list for the framing of the building. A gracious neighbour from Quick East Road sent out a list of the needs to all the people in the Quick area who were on her email list, which was a great help.

The equipment supplier from Houston donated the use of an excavator, which the friend from Houston operated. The excavator was delivered onsite, and the larger pieces of metal were picked up and put into the metal bins. The site was prepared. A house was to be built!

Questions to Consider

1. Is "doing to others" doing what they would want done for themselves? Eg. Is Jesus telling us we should give money to everyone who asks for it?

2. What do you think it means?

3. Why is it difficult to recognize the needs of others in similar circumstances to our own?

4. Why do you think Jesus said, "Do to others whatever you would like them to do to you. This is the essence of all that is taught in the law and the prophets" (Matthew 7:12)?

Chapter 5

COMPASSIONATE COMMUNITY

Various people from around the Bulkley Valley asked how they could help Eleanor. So with materials list in hand, we asked them if they would like to participate in helping rebuild her house.

We went to the sawmills and asked if they could donate a lift of lumber. The mills in Smithers and Houston didn't have anything in their budget for this, but Eleanor's caring neighbours on Highway 16 were able to get the lumber at discounted rates, as they were both employed at one of the mills. They donated a lift of lumber to boot. It was encouraging that at the same time, others donated money toward the house, some specifically mentioning they would like it to go toward the lumber.

We approached a gravel supply and construction company in Smithers, and as soon as we mentioned the project, the owner said that it was a worthy cause and he would supply all the gravel we needed. He also offered to deliver it at no charge.

The building inspectors approved the plans and said they were only interested in inspecting the house, and the existing septic system would do.

Seeing the amazing commitment of the community, and after going over the plans and costs, some of the directors of a local Christian ministry approached businesses and asked if they would like to participate in this wonderful, quickly-expanding community endeavour.

- A lumber supplier in Smithers committed to all the plywood.
- A hardware store in Smithers committed to supplying all the paint.
- An insulation company in Telkwa offered to donate all the insulation.
- A building supplier in Telkwa offered the roofing and siding for the house. They thanked us for asking, because they saw the need and, from previous experience, knew what it was like to take on such a project.
- A Telkwa concrete company donated all the concrete.

One day we were driving along Highway 16 near Quick when we were stopped by a neighbour who was a concrete placer. He asked when we were going to start on Eleanor's house, as he had all the forms ready to go for the foundation. Things were coming together!

- We spoke to a Smithers truss and millwork company, and they committed to supplying all the outside doors.
- A generous glass company in Smithers supplied all the windows.
- A local retired engineer graciously designed trusses that would be made onsite.

At a certain point, we presented some figures to a local Christian ministry. There were enough commitments to cover everything but $25,000 of it (although when we were done, we realized it was more like $35,000). We knew that more people wanted to help out, and the best-case scenario would be having the whole house paid for by volunteer labour, donated materials, and financial contributions.

The ministry decided to open the way for people to donate toward the project and receive a tax receipt for their donation, if they so desired. They also committed to any overruns, up to $10,000, to be paid out of their benevolent fund. This was the go-ahead. The house was to be built, no matter what. The commitment was made! Knowing the need to have a knowledgeable person heading up the project, the ministry's board of directors hired a local general contractor to oversee the building of the house from beginning to end. He offered to do this at half his normal rate.

We called my friend in Houston and had the general contractor onsite as we dug the hole for the foundation. The concrete placer and his crew came in and set up the forms. Before we knew it, the concrete had been poured and we had a foundation for the house.

Compassionate Community

COMMUNITY

Rikki Schierer/Interior News

A work group gets started on building a new home for Eleanor Bennett after hers burned down in a wildfire last August.

Eleanor Bennett set to get home rebuilt

By Cameron Orr
Smithers/Interior News

After a year of living in a friend's home, Eleanor Bennett is ready to move back into her own new home after her last house burned in a small wildfire last August.

Last August, Bennett was checking on her door during a strong bout of wind and saw flames moving up her acreage towards her house.

It was later determined that a tree had fallen on a power pole which sparked the flames.

Since then she has been allowed to live at a friend's home not far away, but soon her friend is coming back to town and she needs a place of her own.

That's where the community of Quick has come in and work is underway to get a brand new home up and ready to move in by the end of June.

The contact for the project is Ken Penner and he's been busy trying to secure donations of money and supplies.

"It's just coming together," he said, which has been well underway for weeks now.

A class from Houston Christian School even came by one day and collected left over debris from the property to get it ready for a new foundation.

Bennett picked out a general floor plan for the house herself

from the Internet and Penner said John De-Witt put it together into a solid plan that has passed approval by the building inspector.

Penner said there is about $25,000 worth of material they still need to come in before everything can be finished but they didn't let that hold up the start of construction.

A partial list of things they still need are electrical supplies to wire the home, some plumb-

ing supplies, a pedestal bathroom sink, bathroom cabinet and trim for the house.

They could also use more hands in carpentry and in plumbing.

Eleanor has lived on the property for 43 years, and her home had only one previous owner when she took possession of it.

She said past owners lost their title to the property and she made a move to purchase it when it

reverted to Crown Land. She didn't get all the acreage it was initially however, only getting five acres out of the 80 available around it.

Despite losing her home, she has kept a high spirited attitude through the whole ordeal.

"You've got to think positive," she said.

If anyone has anything to offer, including money, they can call Ken Penner at 250-846-5439. Tax receipts are available.

Newspaper article June 1, 2011.
(Article courtesy Interior News)

35

Questions to Consider

1. Is it reasonable to expect more contributions from larger corporations than from individuals? Is it reasonable to expect donations from anyone? Why?

2. Could it be that the one who gave the smallest amount gave the most? See Mark 12:41–44.

3. According to Jesus, "It is more blessed to give than to receive" (Acts 20:35b). Who is the most blessed, the giver or the receiver? In what way?

4. With all this in mind, is it wise to compare who gave what and how much?

Chapter 6

MY PROJECT, NOT YOURS!

At one point early on in the project, one of the suppliers' delivery workers asked the general contractor who the materials were to be billed to. Surprised and not knowing what to say, the general contractor phoned me from the building site. He firmly indicated that he did not want it on his bill. What should we do?

I was sure that the owner of the company supplying the material had said that he would contribute it as a donation, but with this question, doubts came into my mind. *It had only been a verbal commitment. Maybe commitments should have been followed up with signed statements. Would that have been more binding? Had I not made it clear that this was a project of volunteers and donated materials? Had he*

changed his mind?[*] *Who was going to pay the substantial sum?*
The general contractor voiced some hesitation about being
involved in the project if this was going to become a pattern.
We decided that they should bill it to my account until we
got things straightened out.

For some reason, this little incident stunned me and filled
me with doubts and fear. Questions swirled through my
mind: *Had we gone ahead with something that was going to
come back and sting us? Would all those who had already made
commitments to labour and supplies back out and leave us in
the lurch? Would I have to take out a mortgage on my house to
cover expenses? What were we to do now?*

Then the thought of going to God in prayer entered
my mind. Shaken and desperate, I got down on my knees
and brought it all before the Lord: "Lord, were we wrong
to proceed in this way? Did I misunderstand? Was I being
presumptuous? What should we do?"

Suddenly, in the middle of the doubts, questions, com-
plaints, and petitions, I received a strong impression. I've
never heard the audible voice of God, and this was not
an audible voice. My eardrums weren't vibrating, but my
heart was!

"This is not your project," I sensed. "It is mine. Trust me,
I will take care of it and show you and others my provision.
Just obey me; it will be okay. Don't worry!" This was the
essence of the very strong impression I got.

---

[*] Incidentally, the supplier did understand what was happening and gladly
donated thousands of dollars of materials completely free of cost.

There was no more doubt in my mind. It had dissipated just like the morning fog when the rising summer sun shines through. The message was clear: We were to proceed and let God take care of things, even the impossible!

With my heart still resonating with this encouraging word, I promptly phoned the general contractor, informing him of this strong impression. He, being a man of faith, was familiar with hearing from God in this way. I could tell that his heart started to resonate too. His answer was immediate and definitive. This was all he needed to hear; he was in for the long haul. There was never a doubt whose project it was after that!

This was only the beginning. God had great wonders ahead for all of us to see.

Questions to Consider

1. Have you ever started something and then wondered how you would finish it? Did you ever complete it?

2. Do you believe that God can speak to us today? How does he do this?

3. Have you ever had a God moment when you felt God was speaking to you? How did it make you feel?

4. If this has happened to you, did you share it with others?

5. How would you know for certain if God was speaking to you?

6. Would God ever contradict his written Word the Bible?

Chapter 7

POWER PLAY

As the fire had started from a tree blowing over and landing on a power line owned by the power company, we had considered, with advice from the helpful lawyer, if we should sue the company for the loss of Eleanor's house. Even though Eleanor had contacted the power company on numerous occasions in the past about trees being too near the line, we decided that it wasn't worth the effort to sue.

When we contacted the power company, they told us that they wanted a reconnection fee of $500. They also said we needed to put in a power pole between the house and the pole across the road, because the rules had changed and they could no longer run lines farther than one hundred feet. The distance to the house was about 120 feet. Then they gave us a bill for around $2,100 to cover engineering the pole site and putting up a new transformer. This made me really upset, as it just wasn't right. Subsequently when Eleanor phoned the office to get the ball rolling with the power company, she told the receptionist that she was hooking up again because her house had burned down due to a forest fire caused by their power line. The lady said she would mark this on the bill and that Eleanor wouldn't be charged the $500.

This left the $2,100 still outstanding for the engineering and the transformer. I got the phone number of the man in charge of customer relations and spoke to him. He was very polite and sounded sympathetic but said there was nothing he could do, as this was the power company's policy. The fee would have to be paid or there would be no electricity from them.

While we were working on the forms for the concrete, I mentioned the situation with the power company to the ministry board chairman, who was working beside me at the time. We were both disgusted that they would do such a thing. Then the chairman said that he'd talked to a lawyer friend of his who'd indicated that he'd be willing to proceed with a lawsuit against the power company pro bono, if that's what Eleanor wanted. It sounded enticing to make them pay, but something inside of me said, *What's happening here on Eleanor's house is too good of a thing to ruin with a lawsuit.*

At that very moment, I had a flashback to an experience I'd had some months earlier while visiting a friend on his deathbed at the hospital in Smithers. Entering the room, I immediately noticed an acquaintance of mine who was speaking intently with a local lawyer who was sitting beside his bed. I walked past them as they were obviously deep in conversation. After a brief visit and prayer with my friend, as I was leaving the room, the acquaintance in the other bed interrupted the conversation with his lawyer and asked me if I would pray for him as well.

"Sure," I said, "how about right now?"

"No, no," he said, "I mean when you're at home, pray for me."

Indicating in the affirmative, I asked him if he believed in prayer, and he said, "Yes, it's my life."

Then I turned to the lawyer who was listening to our conversation and asked him if he believed in prayer. He looked a bit surprised but quickly answered, "Yes, I do. Pray ... pray and sue."

What kind of an answer is that? I thought. It just didn't sound right to me—pray and sue. The two don't mix. Walking out of that hospital room, I wondered, *What real significance did that conversation have for life?*

It proved to have great significance, because when the board chairman and I were discussing suing the power company, it came clearly into my mind. I knew immediately that it wouldn't be right to sue the power company. Things were coming together so well with this community project, and a lawsuit would only give such a sweet thing a very bitter taste. But it was really up to Eleanor.

The next day I phoned the community relations fellow at the power company and unloaded my frustration on him. I told him that I had to tell somebody, and he was probably the best one to unload on right now. I expressed to him that it was a disgrace for the power company to add grief upon grief for Eleanor. Was it not enough that her place had burned down and she'd lost everything? And now they were going to charge her these exorbitant fees to hook her up again. I also told him that the community recognized that the power company had a responsibility to do something to help out, especially when it was a fire that started from their power line. I mentioned that a lawyer had offered to sue them, as he felt they were responsible for this tragic situation, but that we weren't interested in lawsuits unless Eleanor wanted to pursue one. Closing the conversation, he said that he would look into it, declaring that they did not want a lawsuit either.

A few days later he phoned and said that they were dropping all the fees and we should apply for a time-limited grant that might be available for improving the efficiency of the house. I looked up the website he gave me and found that the grant couldn't be given to the Christian ministry, as it was a religious organization. We thought that perhaps the local women's institute could apply. We spoke to one of their members, and she spoke to their committee, and they applied. They got the grant and gave it to Eleanor.

Now the power company wanted us to put in that pole I mentioned earlier. This was another unforeseen expense at the beginning of the project. We spoke to a worker at the power company office about this, because we needed specifications for it. He suggested a pole installation company from Terrace that might be able to help. When we contacted them, they immediately said they would like to install the pole at no charge. One Monday, we went to the project site, and there was the pole standing with an anchor and all the rigging, ready for the electricity to be hooked up. We never did meet anyone from the pole installation company face to face, but they had left their kind footprint on Eleanor's yard!

Incidentally, one of the employees at the power company phoned at a later date and said he would like to help by purchasing a hot water tank for the house. This was miraculous, God was obviously at work in this wonderful community!

Questions to Consider

1. What do you think the power company's responsibility was toward Eleanor?

2. Why do you think the power company changed its mind about charging Eleanor?

3. What do you think about the statement "pray and sue" in general and in this context?

4. Why do you think the power company had a policy to not give grants to religious organizations? Do you think this is right?

5. Have you ever had a flashback to a previous incident that helped you discern what to do in a later situation?

Chapter 8

A LITTLE BIT OF HEAVEN

While the materials miraculously came in just when required, volunteer labour and funding were still needed. Many generous donors gave financially, and these funds allowed us to hire the general contractor. He volunteered all of his tools and only charged half his rate. Obviously, he also forfeited any other work that might have come his way while he was working on this project. He had also volunteered his time to design the house and donated most of the interior doors, including the closet doors. He made an invaluable contribution to help this dream come true.

Day to day, amazingly, numerous workers volunteered their time and showed up just as needed and with the expertise for the particular jobs at hand.

One day, a lady phoned and asked who we were and why we were doing this. I informed her of the overwhelming benevolence of the local community, as well as the compulsion by many to do as Jesus had said "Do to others". She asked what religion we were, and I explained that most of us were Christians, but many others were helping out as well. She said that her heart was warmed by this outreach of compassion, as she had nearly been burned out of her house at one time too. Then she asked if she, as a Buddhist, could help out in any way. I indicated that this was an opportunity for anyone to help as they felt they could. She offered to help paint when that opportunity arose. She was such an encouragement when she came to apply her skills!

A fellow who said he was an atheist helped with framing, some local men poured the concrete, and others finished the floor in the crawl space. A Christian missionary on furlough came along with some friends for a few days. He was also a carpenter, and the general contractor was able to assign a portion of the floor and framing to them. All these people together made for a remarkably productive work crew!

A local Christian man from Quick came to help out for at least three weeks. One day I asked him if he was enjoying the project, and he quickly answered that it was just like a "little bit of heaven" to be working on the house.

Every day we had enough supplies and people to keep the building progressing at an incredibly efficient pace. The mix of local people and those far and wide made it a very special project. Each individual played their part in helping Eleanor get into her new home.

Questions to Consider

1. What are your thoughts on having people from various religious backgrounds working together on the project?

2. Why do you think the local Christian man said that it was "a little bit of heaven" for him to volunteer his time?

Chapter 9

GOD'S GRACIOUS SUPPLY

The Electrical

Another serious test arose when we approached a local electrician friend about the wiring. He graciously committed to doing all the work to install it if we would supply the materials. We'd assumed the materials would cost around $1,500, but when we brought up the subject, he said it would be more like $3,000 or $4,000. This was a bit of a shock, as we hadn't counted on this extra cost or included it in the total estimate. We hadn't properly researched it.

At the advice of our electrician friend, I approached a local wholesale electrical supplier. The manager was acutely aware of the fire, as he spent a considerable amount of time hunting in the Quick area. He was very sympathetic and said he would look into what he could do. When he asked what we needed, I told him that our electrician would have a better idea. Some weeks later, when we were almost ready to do the wiring, the electrician texted me and asked us to contact the manager, as they had a proposal for supplying the materials. When I spoke to the manager, he simply informed me that they would supply all the electrical materials, everything, no charge. It was covered! The electrician and his capable crew came in at various stages throughout the project and did a wonderful job. Whatever they needed was supplied by the electrical supplier. We were amazed at the magnificent way the good Lord supplied everything through so many wonderful people. Though the house was progressing nicely, we still had many pleasant miracles to experience before it was complete.

The Plumbing

One evening we got a call from a local building contractor who had heard of the project and wanted to donate all the insulation. When I informed him that the insulation was already donated, he asked what else was needed. I informed him that the plumbing materials still needed to be covered, and he said he had a running bill at the building supply in Telkwa and that we could charge whatever we needed to his account. When I asked him what the limit was for expenditures, he chuckled and said not to worry, he would keep track and let us know when it was too much! We never heard from him again!

A Smithers plumbing and heating business offered to install all the plumbing. They went to the building supply in Telkwa and picked up whatever they needed to complete the job, billing everything to the building contractor. All their workers graciously volunteered their time.

Questions to Consider

1. What is the difference between compassion and sympathy? What were these people expressing to Eleanor?

2. What did Jesus show when he fed the multitude of people in Matthew 15:32-39?

3. Even though we had made a mistake in our estimate, the needed electrical materials were still graciously supplied. What does this say about God's grace when we are willing to obey him, even if we make a mistake or misstep in the process?

4. The Noah Webster's 1828 dictionary defines grace as: "the free unmerited love and favor of God." How does this apply to this project?

5. What risks did the building contractor incur by letting us charge the plumbing supplies to his account? What did this action say about his commitment to the project? His commitment to God?

Chapter 10

MULTICOLOURED

I met with the ministry board chairman one day to pray and to discuss the various needs for Eleanor's house. As part of the conversation, we agreed to approach a local drywall and paint contractor about getting some drywall. After the conclusion of this conversation, I met with a friend for coffee at a local restaurant. As we walked into the restaurant, guess who was sitting there having lunch? The drywall and paint contractor we'd just talked about! We sat with him and explained the project. Without hesitation, he offered to supply and install all the drywall.

Another neighbourhood drywall contractor committed to mudding the drywall and helping with the painting. He was very excited about working on the same project as his competition. All the work was top notch and done efficiently.

Many calls came in offering practical help with the labour. One call regarding painting stands out. A group of neighbours from down the road, and the gracious Buddhist lady mentioned earlier, quickly applied bright coloured paint to the newly constructed walls. Previous to this, I had approached a good friend of mine who owned a local hardware store about providing some paint at a bit of a discount. He offered all the paint for free, and his lovely wife helped Eleanor select the best paint and match the colours.

The helpful neighbour from down Highway 16 stayed in high gear throughout the project, helping to procure materials, insulate, and paint. The house was taking shape and becoming a reality. A miracle was happening before our eyes as hope literally came out of the ashes of despair!

Questions to Consider

1. Do you think it was coincidence or a Divine appointment that we met up with the drywall and paint contractor just after praying and discussing his possible involvement? What are the odds of this happening, especially considering his response?

2. The helpful neighbour showed up consistently to do whatever she could, even the most menial jobs, like insulating the crawl space. Would you like to live next door to someone like this?

3. What does Jesus teach about our "neighbour" in the parable of the Good Samaritan (Luke 10:25–37)?

Chapter 11

KITCHEN ESSENTIALS

Our primary goal was to get Eleanor a roof over her head. In discussions with the general contractor, we agreed that we would look at finishing the inside once we knew how much we could afford. In hindsight, I'm embarrassed to say that we even discussed putting up some two-by-four cupboards with a plywood top and cloth sheets to close them in. But God had different plans. He was going to teach us how wonderfully he wants to take care of his own, and he used some generous people to fulfill his desire to bless Eleanor!

I'd been looking for cost estimates on cupboards. The general contractor, in consultation with Eleanor, had drawn up a plan of the cupboard and countertop layout. There weren't many cupboards, which revealed Eleanor's practical and frugal nature. She didn't want a palace, just a functional place with a roof over her head. With the plans for the cupboards in hand, I went into a local shop in Telkwa that sold many things at a lower price than did other stores. I asked how much that type of a cupboard would cost, and the owner mentioned that they only had high-end cupboards. After he asked some questions and looked at the plans, he came up with a ballpark figure. *This is out of our league*, I thought. *Too fancy*. As we talked, I mentioned who the cupboard was for and the amazing response from the community so far.

A few days later we got a call from the owner of the store, asking for the plans. He was going to order the cupboards and donate them free of charge! Wow, what a surprise! Benevolent people, I would say.

Next, we needed the countertops. My sister and brother from Terrace who used to live near Eleanor had recently remodelled their kitchen and had some mint-condition countertops left over. They wanted to donate them to Eleanor's house, and all we had to do was pick them up. Some generous people brought them on their way through. We measured them up and found that they would fit perfectly. Even the opening for the sink was already cut out, exactly where we had previously planned and had already installed the plumbing. The corner was cut in the exact spot that it needed to be. All we had to do was cut twelve inches off one end. The general contractor and I looked at each other amazed at how God was bringing it all together!

God had another amazing miracle to show us concerning the countertop. The general contractor went to a cabinet shop in Smithers to get the twelve inches cut off. He wondered how the newly cut end could be finished, as the countertop had been bought in Terrace, and the chances of finding a matching piece of Arborite to finish the end would be almost impossible. After the end was cut off, he asked the fellow at the cabinet shop if they had a piece lying around that might match somewhat. They looked in the bin of ends and pieces, and lo and behold, there was a piece that matched exactly, lying right on the top of all the rest of the scraps! They trimmed it to size and glued it on, just as if it had all been preplanned! Coincidence, some might say, but I don't think so. It was definitely the hand of God. He wanted Eleanor to have a first-class countertop.

When the cupboards arrived, they matched exactly with the countertop. These were high-end, soft-close cupboards. It's embarrassing to think that we had once considered two-by-fours with cloth sheets. God is good. He cares for us in every detail!

The extravagance of God's love was again shown through a group of truck drivers and workers at the concrete supply company. When the footings were being poured, one of the truckers approached me and asked what Eleanor still needed for her kitchen. I had in mind such things as cutlery and dishes, but Eleanor was standing nearby, so I introduced the trucker to her. She asked Eleanor what she'd like to have for her kitchen, and Eleanor responded that she'd never had a dishwasher and would really like one. To my embarrassment, I thought this might be somewhat extravagant, because we were still wondering how most of the more essential supplies and labour would materialize. The trucker glanced at me, and I thought she was thinking the same thing. But when I got home that evening, there was a message on my telephone from the lady trucker. I called her and she explained that when she heard that Eleanor had never had a dishwasher, she knew she would make sure she got one. She discussed it with the other truckers and workers at the concrete supply plant, and they all chipped in to get her a dishwasher. The compassion of these wonderful people just melted my heart and reminded me of the words recorded in the scriptures: "… you don't have what you want because you don't ask God for it" (James 4:2b).

Toward the end of the project, a generous neighbour bought a new electric stove to complement the kitchen.

Questions to Consider

1. When planning the house, we calculated everything as economically as possible, taking into consideration the lower or medium end products. We even considered using two-by-fours to finish the kitchen if needed, yet high end cupboards were graciously given. What does this say to you about God's love for Eleanor? For us?

2. What are the odds of the countertop being almost exactly what was needed?

3. Do you think that God had something to do with the piece of scrap Arborite that was found? What would be the odds of this happening by coincidence?

4. My thoughts and the thoughts of the trucker were completely different. What does this say about us reading other people's thoughts or body language?

5. To me, it seemed extravagant to talk about a dishwasher when we were still wondering how to make ends meet on the basics of the building. Yet the heart of the trucker was moved to supply this for Eleanor. What lessons can we learn from this?

Chapter 12

A TABLE TO DINE ON

The Flooring

The neighbour from across Highway 16 had some laminate flooring available from a project he never got to. The general contractor estimated that it would cover something like one and a half bedrooms. The neighbour farther down Highway 16 also had some laminate flooring left over from a previous project.

If you know anything about laminate flooring, you know that there are many different manufacturers, styles, thicknesses, and colours. What are the chances of these two different batches of flooring, bought in different places at different times, matching up? "Almost nil," the general contractor and I agreed. We put little stock in being able to use any of this flooring, but when we compared the packages, we saw that they were from the same manufacturer. They were only slightly different in colour, and they were the same thickness. They even snapped together perfectly! And there was more than enough to finish the living room and the bedrooms. The colours were so close that they could be alternated to make a very beautiful floor. When it was done, it was beautiful indeed!

Rather than work out the odds of this happening by chance, I will give God the credit! It was overwhelmingly obvious that he wanted this flooring put down in Eleanor's house! Another flooring supplier from Smithers offered the linoleum for the kitchen at half price.

The Kitchen Table

A generous young couple donated a brand-new, solid wood kitchen table. We just had to take it out of the box and put it together. When we had the table upside down on the floor, fastening the legs to it, Eleanor looked up and said, "Today is August 18. It's been exactly one year since my place burned down. One year ago, I was watching everything go up in flames." Now she had her own house and a roof over her head, in which she was already living! And she had a solid wood kitchen table to dine on.

The Kitchen Chairs

We're not done with the table yet. It came without chairs, as the generous young couple who had donated it needed them. Eleanor only had one plastic chair to sit on.

A few weeks later, a generous lady called Eleanor to ask her if she needed some chairs. She had bought a brand-new table and chairs set but only needed the table. You won't believe this, but the chairs were a perfect match for the table. They had come from the same manufacturer and were the same model and colour as the donated table. I wouldn't have believed it if I hadn't seen it! God had his hand in this, no doubt.

The community certainly had come together. A miracle was happening. Actually, it was a series of many miracles that happened as each person opened up their heart to face a tragedy together! One year after the fire, Eleanor was able to eat on her own table in her own house!

Questions to Consider

1. What would have happened if one of Eleanor's neighbours had thought that their contribution of laminate flooring was too small or trivial to give?

2. Does it seem significant that exactly a year after the fire totally destroyed her house, Eleanor was eating at her own table in her own house on her own property?

3. It was impossible for Eleanor to remember who had given what, and with so many to thank, this was overwhelming to her. She was thanking the Lord every day! If you were in her shoes, who would be the first one you would thank?

4. Practicality would say any chairs will do, yet she got the exact match of four chairs for her table—room for her, some family, and friends! We may have been able to order a matching set, but no human did. Could it have been God's plan?

Chapter 13

FINISHING TOUCHES

The Eavestrough and Siding

One of the calls I received during the construction of the house was from an eavestrough supplier from Telkwa. He had previously worked with Eleanor at the greenhouses down Highway 16 and felt compelled to help out. Without any solicitation whatsoever, he insisted that he would install the soffits and the eavestrough when the house was ready for it. When the time came, he showed up with his friend, and they quickly and professionally installed it. Later he told me that this was one of the most precious times in his Christian life, when all the people got together to help out Eleanor with her house!

One day somebody dropped off some siding that had been lying around their place, left over from a previous project. Much of this siding was still in the original packing boxes. It was a different colour than that supplied by the building supplier in Telkwa, but it was of the same type, so with a little ingenuity, the two were utilized to make a beautiful two-tone cladding for the house!

The Landscaping

As the project came to completion, the general contractor used his backhoe to landscape around the house. Eleanor loved to plant things, but at this point there wasn't much good topsoil to finish off the landscaping. The rancher down Highway 16 noticed this and offered to supply some top-notch garden soil to help with the finishing touches outside. Another neighbour who was a landscaper used his Bobcat to spread it out and tidy things up.

The Interior News   Wednesday, February 8, 2012   www.interior-news.com   A5

The house a community built

Eleanor's back in her own home

By Cameron Orr
Quick/Interior News

A fire is what rapidly destroyed a Quick woman's home when a spark from a transformer ignited surrounding trees.

It was community spirit which put it back again.

Eleanor Bennett can now put her feet up in a brand new home, which was made possible thanks to numerous donations of time and material to create a new, two bedroom bungalow.

The final touch on the house was finished on Aug. 17, 2011. That is one year, minus a day, from when her home was brought down.

It was a testing time for Eleanor, who was baptized in the Skeena River in Thornhill just three days before the fire.

She and others consider the fire an act of God.

"A few people said, 'well, it was God's way of telling you to move on and start fresh'," she said.

She said she has changed her ways since, and has made it her mission to not collect so many possessions moving forward.

The house is a bit smaller than the one she used to live in, which helps her to that purpose.

She's happy in this new home, the effort of numerous people. Now, she can see the highway from her windows, as the home is positioned closer to the road than she was before.

Eleanor has a list of donors about three pages long and she illustrates how generous the community was because she only knows about half of a page's worth of people who contributed.

Ken Penner is a close friend of Bennett and got to know her through some in-home church services at a mutual friend's house. He is the one who baptized her in Thornhill shortly before the fire.

When she lost her house in the fire he is the one who set the gears in motion to organize the effort to get her house rebuilt.

A lot of things fell into place in the rebuild.

For instance, he said that they were donated some laminate floors, but there wasn't enough to entirely finish the kitchen.

Separate from this, someone won an auction on some flooring for the home, and brought it to Ken and Eleanor. When they put the two floorings together, turns out they were a great fit, both from the same brand.

The design was even similar to each other and Ken said that it actually looks better now than if it was just one design.

He knows nothing would have happened if it was just him and is thankful for so much help that came their way. It was, he thinks, a divine plan.

"It's not about me. God wanted Eleanor to have a house."

> ### A few people said, 'well, it was God's way of telling you to move on and start fresh'.
> — *Eleanor Bennett*

Above, submitted. Below, Cameron Orr photo
Above, Eleanor Bennett's new home. Below, the smoking site the day after her home burned in 2010.

Newspaper article, February 8, 2012
(Photos and article courtesy Interior News)

Questions to Consider

1. When past acquaintances and fellow workers experience tragedy, could it be an opportunity to help out?

2. When Jesus said "It is more blessed to give than to receive" (Acts 20:35b) Could it be that part of what he meant was having the peace of knowing you did the right thing?

3. The rancher down Highway 16 offered the topsoil without even being asked. What does this say about his care for Eleanor?

Chapter 14

ENOUGH TO FINISH!

Eleanor had moved in. All had gone well, amazingly smooth, almost without a wrinkle. This was remarkable! Only God could have orchestrated such a compassionate community response. What had begun as a tragedy had turned out to be a blessing!

We had a gathering at the house to which all the known participants were invited. It was a wonderful time, as they were able to see the house they'd had a part in building. It was exciting to meet many of the people there. Overwhelmed and with tears in her eyes, Eleanor thanked all for their help. We prayed together to thank God for what he had done, for without him it would not have been possible!

The general contractor moved his equipment back home. It looked as if we were done. Mission accomplished! We were all delighted, as the job was completed! Then the water problems appeared—many mysterious water problems. It was discouraging to say the least, much like a deflated balloon after a birthday party, but I would be remiss if I didn't include this part of the story. So hang on, there is more! Possibly the greatest lesson to be learned came at the end.

We had hooked up the water lines, and the water flowed for a bit. After a while, it became murky, and then dirty, and then it stopped altogether. We thought it might be a problem with the well, which was 250 metres from the house. We pulled the lid off the well and saw that it was full to the top with water. The gracious neighbour across the road rented a water pump and helped to pump it out. We pulled up the foot-valve. It was stuck open, so we replaced it with a high quality new one, kindly supplied by a water plumbing business in Smithers. After priming the pump again, we still had no water. Eleanor had a few funds left in her special bank account, so she bought a new pump. We installed it but still no water. We asked advice from a retired plumber from Smithers, who loaned us a different kind of pump. We tried it, but to no avail.

Finally, after some serious prayer on the matter and advice from the retired plumber, the general contractor and I decided that it must be a problem with the water line. We thought we might have to replace the 250 metres of the line. He brought his backhoe from Smithers, and we started digging from the house to the well. We soon found that the line had separated from a fitting on an elbow when the waterline was inadvertently pulled by the excavator when we first excavated the basement. We put in new line to that point and hooked everything up. It worked! Water to the house! Water pressures were set, and we were done! Thank the Lord!

About a week or so later, Eleanor noticed water sitting near the water tank behind the toilet. I discovered that the fittings weren't tightened and water had leaked from there. A simple fix it seemed, yet a few days later, she found water beside her dishwasher. The general contractor found a loose fitting there too and tightened it up. After the water was on for about two or three weeks, she found water leaking into her crawl space. Upon closer examination, we noticed that some water had seeped under the linoleum and the flooring in the living room. Following the water to the source, I found three compression rings on the Pex pipe that had not been compressed, so I got a compression tool and tightened them. The water leaks stopped.

The floor was soaked and the air in the house was saturated with water vapour, which steamed up the windows. To keep mold from forming in the house, the general contractor pulled out all the kitchen appliances, cupboards, linoleum, and the living room flooring that was wet and damaged. Windows were opened and heaters and fans set up to move the air and accelerate drying. We left it to air out in this way for about a week until everything completely dried out. Then with amazing efficiency, the general contractor reinstalled the linoleum, kitchen cupboards, and appliances. We had enough laminate left over to replace the damaged living room flooring! All was done, with no more leaks. Now Eleanor had the house to herself!

I wondered why it had happened. Nobody purposely tried to sabotage the project, and everyone was so helpful. I think that stuff just happens—things beyond our control, like the pipe disconnecting from the fitting. As humans, we also make mistakes sometimes that can come back to haunt us, like the uncompressed compression rings that were over-looked on the pipeline. But I think there's a deeper lesson here. After a high, there is always, somewhere down the road, a low. When stuff goes wrong, for whatever reason, we need to persevere. The work of God and his intervention is often the most obvious when we come to the end of our-selves. We were tempted to throw up our hands and come up with excuses like "I can't do anything here" or "I'm not a plumber, let someone else figure it out." But the real solu-tion was to ask God for patience and wisdom, bear down, and methodically figure it out as he gave us strength and insight to do so.

I know when I come to the end of my rope, God is still there. He promised that he would meet us and give rest to the weary and burdened. He is enough for us to finish well, no matter what the circumstances! When Eleanor lost every-thing, it seemed quite desperate. But in the end, God called a compassionate community to help her find her way out of that spot. He supplied everything that was needed. The supplies and the donated funds were all used, everything was paid for, and Eleanor has a house she can enjoy as long as God sees fit!

I am glad I had the privilege to play a very small part of being a caring community in the face of tragedy!

Questions to Consider

———

1. When everything seems to go wrong and events don't go as we would like, does that mean God is not involved?

2. Is this a time to give up or a time to persevere?

3. How can we know when to give up and when to persevere?

Chapter 15

JUST IN TIME

After the house was completed, I was chatting with the general contractor, and he made some significant comments. He said it was a great blessing to work on the project, and that he had never worked on a project like it before. Usually he would order much of the materials well before the time they were needed and would have them all stocked up and ready to go. On this project, there was very little stockpiled, as the materials arrived just when they were needed. During the building process, he would often ask me where the next material was, as they would be needing it soon. I'd tell him that we didn't have it yet, so we'd have to trust that God would supply the need. The materials always arrived in time, and no one ever had to wait for the needed supplies!

When sharing this particular miracle with a brother who has training in finances, he enlightened me that this was called JIT (Just in Time inventory). He explained that JIT is the most efficient and cost-effective form of inventory control for any business. It's what every president, manager, and supervisor would like to see happen. If a car manufacturing facility can get the parts they're assembling just as they're needed, this will cut inventory costs, inventory storage, and inventory management in stocking materials. This is precisely what happened on Eleanor's house! There was very little in materials that we had to purchase ahead of time, so very little piled up around the house! It was a classic example of Just in Time inventory.

This had nothing to do with the expertise of all those involved but was by the direction of God! He brought the materials at just the right time! The general contractor said that if he had done it in the usual way, he would have had all the materials stocked up on site well before he needed them. This time God was the manager, and he had it planned before it was ever done. He had certain individuals all around the area who would heed his call and provide what was needed, Just in Time.

This not only pertained to the materials but also to the labor. On a typical project, the contractor would usually have his trained crew of a few men come and work until the job was done. On this project, people came and went on a seemingly casual basis. However, whenever there was a need, someone was there, untrained or trained, but always willing to do what was needed. The contractor commented that this was one of the fastest and most smoothly run projects he had ever done! It was done far faster and more efficiently than if he'd done it in the conventional way!

Questions to Consider

1. How many people are usually involved in building a small dwelling such as Eleanor's? How many people were involved in Eleanor's house project? (For a partial list, look at the list in the Appendix at the end of this book.)

2. How would so many people being involved change the complexity of the project?

3. If we didn't know where the materials or labour were necessarily coming from, how could the project proceed?

4. In the normal course of events, what would one call a project run in this way?

5. Considering God's supernatural intervention, what would one call it?

6. Considering the whole picture and the fact that in the end it was a good example of Just in Time inventory management, who do you think was the true manager of this project? Who should we be thankful to? Who should get all the glory?

Chapter 16

THE VISION

One night during the infant stage of this project, I woke up after having a dream of Eleanor standing beside her house. It was a beautiful little house; she was standing beside it and looking down her driveway and waving. This was encouraging at the time but quickly forgotten when the details of the work involved came upon us. Yet this was exactly what happened! Eleanor has a house. She says it is exceptionally warm, and she is thankful to the Lord and all those who helped her make the impossible possible! After a visit, she can often be seen standing beside her house and waving!

Eleanor's new house!
(Picture courtesy K. Penner)

This dream reminds me of the scripture verse written some 2,900 years ago by the wise King Solomon: "Where there is no vision, the people perish" (Proverbs 29:18a, KJV). Here we have an example of how a community of so many people had a desire and vision to help out in the face of tragedy! With vision like this, what else can happen but the people be blessed to flourish and prosper!

Questions to Consider

1. Where does true vision come from?

2. What happened as everyone's vision for Eleanor came together?

3. Could the house have been built without the help of each one involved?

4. If the house had been covered by insurance and thus built by a contractor, would as many people have been blessed in the process?

5. How would our society be different if everyone always got together to help each other out in the face of tragedy?

Chapter 17

ETERNAL HOME

Throughout this brief recollection of God's wonderful care for Eleanor, it is obvious how he intervened in a tragic situation and rescued in miraculous ways. This was typically done through ordinary people. Neighbours wanted to help and gave of their time and resources. One of the gracious people who helped said that a forest fire had almost burned her house down, which motivated her to do something for Eleanor. Others had different motivations. Would not the world be a better place if this was the norm?

But there is definitely more here, much more than mere human intervention. No human being could have planned for the details to come together in the way they did! It was nothing short of miraculous! One might want to reread this little booklet with this in mind to see more clearly the divine interventions that occurred throughout this beautiful work of God! Every time I think of it, I'm awestruck at the overflowing, intimate love and grace of our heavenly Father, given to us in our need. God obviously supervised this project! Some might think these were coincidences, yet the record speaks for itself!

Sometimes we get so wrapped up with our own lives, looking after ourselves, that we forget the miracles that happen around us every day! Take, for instance, our ability to breathe, or the amazing function of our heart, which beats thousands of times per day to bring life-giving blood and nutrients to every part of our body! We miss the astounding miracle that happens when a little baby is formed in a mother's womb. We even come to believe that this all just happened by chance, by some great lottery in the sky. We look at ourselves and believe we are the only solution to all our problems. No wonder we often feel alone, abandoned, and frustrated! We've missed the very source, the giver and sustainer of life! God open our eyes to see! If he could take care of Eleanor, he can take care of me!

Eleanor's house is finished and has served her well. Though it is a monument of a compassionate community and a very special work of God, it is still only temporary. Could God be interested in eternal things as well as temporary?

When we read the obituaries or attend a funeral, we are reminded of the brevity of life. Since the time of these events, a few of the gracious people involved have already passed away. I am battling with a cancer diagnosis and don't know how it will all work out. God's Word, the Bible, clearly points out, "And just as each person is destined to die once and after that comes judgment," (Hebrews 9:27). We will all die; no one on earth is 150 years old! There is a judgement that will take into account all of our sins. God's Word is clear: "For everyone has sinned; we all fall short of God's glorious standard" (Romans 3:23).

All the good things we've done can never erase the sins we've committed. We all fall short—so short that our sins will separate us from God forever, "For the wages of sin is death" (Romans 6:23a,). This leaves us in an eternal dilemma that we cannot solve ourselves. We are eternally lost if left on our own, yet there is good news, as expressed in the conclusion of this verse: "but the free gift of God is eternal life through Christ Jesus our Lord" (Romans 6:23b). This free gift of God is available to all who will receive it in faith! "But to all who believed him and accepted him, he gave the right to become children of God" (John 1:12); "For God loved the world so much that he gave his one and only Son, so that everyone who believes in him will not perish but have eternal life" (John 3:16)

Though it was truly amazing what God did for Eleanor, it is much more amazing what God has done to make a way for us to dwell forever with him! He didn't do this by sending a bunch of people to prepare this eternal place, but he sent his one and only Son, Jesus Christ, to die on a cruel Roman cross two thousand years ago, to take the death penalty that was due each one of us, so our sins could be forgiven and we could enter into an eternal relationship with him! Yet a gift offered is not ours until we receive it!

Jesus said to His disciples:

> "Don't let your hearts be troubled. Trust in God, and trust also in me. There is more than enough room in my Father's home. If this were not so, would I have told you that I am going to prepare a place for you? When everything is ready, I will come and get you, so that you will always be with me where I am. And you know the way to where I am going."
>
> "No, we don't know, Lord," Thomas said. "We have no idea where you are going, so how can we know the way?"
>
> Jesus told him, "I am the way, the truth, and the life. No one can come to the Father except through me." (John 14:1–6)

Questions to Consider

1. If we pursue helping each other without the intervention of God, how successful might we be? (When thinking on this, one might consider some experiments in this, such as the Soviet Union, China, or North Korea.)

2. Why is it that we often discount, or fail to see, the miraculous when we encounter miracles on a daily basis?

3. When we fail to see the miraculous on a daily basis, does this mean that it is no longer miraculous? Why?

4. If God can miraculously intervene in the building of Eleanor's house, could he intervene in your tragedy and difficulties?

5. What do you think Jesus meant when he said "Trust in God, and trust also in me" and "There is more than enough room in my Father's home"?

6. Many people might think that this story seems too good to be true. How does the evidence of God's

intervention in the pages of this book stand as a reminder of his grace toward us? Does this bear witness to the much greater expression of grace as evidenced by Jesus, the Son of the living God, coming to earth to die for everyone who would turn from going their own way and follow Him?

7. Jesus said, "I am the way, the truth, and the life. No one can come to the Father except through me" (John 14:6). Some say there are many ways to God. Does this statement give room for other ways to God?

8. Should tragedy strike and you die today, would you be ready to meet your maker?

Perhaps you want to be forgiven of your sins, to have a relationship with the Creator of the universe and make your eternal destiny sure. You can do this by turning to God and calling out to him for mercy, and he will wash away every sin and make you his child forever!

The following illustration may be helpful in explaining the truth of God's wonderful Good News to you!

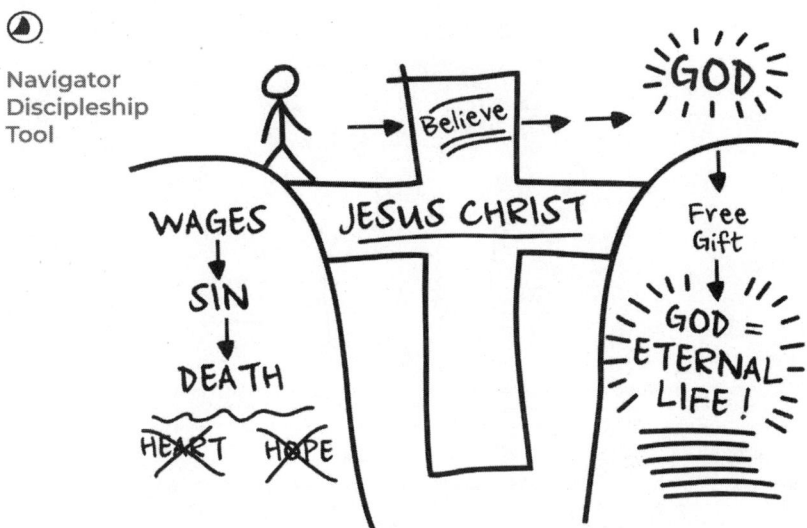

Navigator
Discipleship
Tool

BRIDGE *to* **LIFE**

Some of the oldest questions humankind has been asking are, "How can I know God?" What is He like? What can we do to please Him? How can we get to Heaven? If we work hard enough to be a good enough person will He accept us then? If we do enough religious activities to get His attention, will that do it?

Fortunately for us, the answer is surprisingly simple. The "Gospel" that the Bible talks about literally means, "the Good News," and the news is good indeed!

We have to start at the beginning. In *Genesis 1:26,* when God created the first humans, He said, "Let us make mankind in our image, in our likeness", then God blessed them and spent the days walking and talking with the people He had created. In short, *life was good.*

But why isn't life like that anymore? What happened to mess everything up? This brings us to the second point: when we (humankind) chose to do the opposite of what God told us, sin poisoned the world. *Sin separated us from God, and everything changed. Romans 3:23* says, "For all have sinned and fall short of the glory of God," and in *Isaiah 59:2* we're told,

"your iniquities have separated you from your God; your sins have hidden his face from you so that he will not hear."

This is especially bad news because there is no way for us to get across that gap on our own. We (humankind) have tried to find our way back to God and a perfect world on our own ever since then, and without any luck. We try to get there by being good people, or through religion, money, morality, philosophy, education, or any number of other ways, but eventually we find out that none of it works. "There is a way that seems right to a man, but in the end it leads to death" (*Proverbs 14:12*).

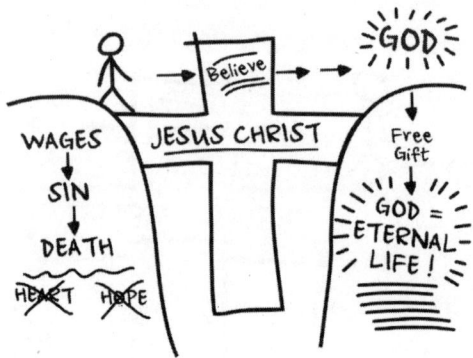

There is only one way to find peace with God, and the Bible says it is through Jesus Christ. We were stranded without any way of getting back to our Creator, and we needed a way to pay for our sins and be clean again so that we could be welcomed back to be with Him. *Romans 5:8* says, "But God demonstrates His own love for us in this: While we were still sinners, Christ died for us." *So this is the Good News*—that even though we were still enemies of God (as one translation says), <u>Jesus came to die on the cross and pay the price for our sins so that we could have a relationship with Him again.</u> *John 3:16* says, "For God so loved the world that He gave His one and only son, that whoever believes in Him shall not perish but have eternal life."

This brings us to the last and most important part. *John 5:24* says, "I tell you the truth, whoever hears my word and believes Him who sent me has eternal life and will not be condemned; <u>he has crossed over from death to life.</u>" Jesus Christ himself even says, "I have come that they may

have life, and have it to the full" (*John 10:10*), and *Romans 5:1* says, "we have peace with God through our Lord Jesus Christ."

So how can I have peace with God, life to the full, and be confident of eternal life like these verses say? First, through an honest prayer to God, I have to admit that I'm not perfect—that I can't escape my sins, and I can't save myself. I follow this admission by believing that Jesus Christ died for me on the cross and rose from the grave, conquering death and sin. Then I invite Jesus Christ to live in me and be the Lord of my life, accepting His free gift of eternal life with Him.

The prayer can go something like this: "*Dear Jesus, I know that I am a sinner and that I need You to forgive me. I know that You died a painful death so that my sins could be washed clean. Thank you. I want to make You the Lord of my life, and I will trust and follow You. Everything I have is Yours now. In Your name, Lord. Amen.*"

There is nothing magical about these words. It's not the words themselves that make things right between you and God—it's whether or not your heart really means it. We know this because in *1 Samuel 16:7*, the Bible says, "The Lord does not look at the things people look at. People look at the outward appearance, but the Lord looks at the heart."

The best part of this whole process is that it doesn't matter how badly we've messed up, Jesus is powerful enough to save anyone from their sins—even the worst of us. *Romans 10:13* says, "Everyone who calls on the name of the Lord will be saved." That's fantastic news—no matter how badly we've messed up, we can place our complete trust in Jesus, and He will wipe all of our sins off the face of the earth. *Jesus is the bridge to life.*

THIS TOOL IS MEANT TO BE SHARED.
To download the Bridge to Life illustration visit navlink.org/bridge

Courtesy Navigators

Appendix

Community in the Face of Tragedy!

Donors[*]

Action Septic Services, *All For Less Store,* All West Glass, *Dave & Ellen Anderson,* Aqua North Plumbing, *B.C. Forest Service,* B.C. Hydro, *Bel Aire Automotive,* Ingrid Bell, *William Beerens,* Rita Bereens, *Dorothy Beerens,* Dave and Bev Berg, *Big Smiles Store,* Roy & Evelyn Boddy, *John & Laurie Boonstra,* Jesse Boonstra, *Rick and Verna Boonstra,* Bulkley Board and Beam, *Bulkley Valley Christian School,* Bulkley Valley Evestroughing, *Bulkley Valley Home Centre,* Kent Cotton, *Jim Cunningham,* D&M Drywall and Painting, *Robert Delege,* Bill deVries, *John and Mary deWit,* Mark deWit, *Stephen deWit,* Sofia deWit, *Doug and Kathy Dobrenski,* Don Giddings

---

[*] These are the donors that we know of, though we did our best in recording, we know there were others that we probably missed. Donations were monetary, labour, advice, and materials.

Law Firm, *E.C. Siding,* Eccol Electric, *Faith Reformed Church,* Franco's Painting and Drywall, *Tom and Arlene George,* Corney Goertzen, *Henk Grasmeyer,* David Gurney, *Leo and Marie Gyger,* Hanken Peak Contracting, *Daryl and Dina Hansen,* Bill Harness, *Dale Harris,* Joe & Alice Hidber, *Nora Higgenson,* Doug and Sarah Hobenshield, *Winslow Hobson,* Mr. Hoffard, *Harry Hofsink,* Guido Holenstein, *Blake Holenstein,* Houston Christian Reformed Church Youth, *Houston Home Hardware,* Huckleberry Mines, *Terry & Sue Huisman,* Aubrey and Roxanne Hunter, *Ted & Bev Huntington,* Interior News, *J & L Contracting,* Nellie Jaarsma, *Thys & Ida Jaarsma,* Carol & Anthony Jackson, *Jody Jackson,* Dieter and Louise Jacobs, *Robin and Cindy Jeffery,* Doug and Cindy Jeffery, *John deWit Contracting,* Art Kerr, *Gordie Kerr,* Harold and SharonKerr, *Milan & Sharon Lacika,* Dwayne Layfield, *Cody Lund,* Jim McGregor, *Henk Meerdink and crew,* Melody Mounfield, *Glen Muir,* Joe Nessman, *North Central Heating Ltd,* North Country Insurance, *North Country Rentals,* Jean Oevermann, *Pacific Truck and Tractor,* Garth Pearson, *Ken & Eunice Penner,* Nathan & Michelle Penner, *Renata Penner,* Cliff Price, *Quick 4H,* Quick Women's Institute, *Fred Reitsma, Roma Richberg,* Denise Rondeau, *Tom Roper,* Round Lake Community Benefit, *Herman Saefkow,* Mac Schat Jr., *Anton and Ellen Seif,* Simpson Controls, *Sip & Stitch Club,* Smithers Home Hardware, *Smithers Lumber Yard,* Stade's Winter Wonderland, *Streetcorners Ministries,* Pete Sutherland, *Fred Tabert,* LeRoy Taylor, *Telkwa Christian Reformed Church,* The Peak Radio Station, *Thermax Insulation,* Total Floors, *Tricon Truss and Millwork,* Twin Rivers Power, *Tony Vandenberg,* Vandenberg Dairy, *Rick and Warren Vandenberg,* Will Verhelst, *Vihar Construction Ltd.,* Magdalene Von Seydlitz, *Doug Walker,* Jesse Walker, *Barbara Walmsley,* Brent Weme, *Joshua Weme,* West Fraser Concrete, *Ivan Widen,* Josette Wier, *Dustin Winthrope,* Steve Winthrope, *Joshua Wisselink,* Joe and Lana Wong, *Woodmere Nursery,* Mike Zantingh.

About the Author

KEN PENNER resides in the beautiful Bulkley Valley of Northwestern British Columbia, Canada. He is happily married; he and his wife Eunice have three children and six grandchildren.

Ken had the honour of being a small part of the amazing work of God expressed through the response of a compassionate community, as recorded in the pages of this book. Though he recorded the events with pen and ink, God is the true Authour. May all the glory go to God and Him alone!

Author enjoys writing, is a regular contributor to local newspapers and has written numerous articles for other publications over the years. This is his first book to be published.